The Man Who Invented Television?

Published by Yarnspinner Publications

First published in 2022
ISBN 9798402783997

The Man Who Invented Television?

The Story of Evered Wigg, a true English Eccentric

by

Geoffrey Brock

Contents

Introduction: The Early Years

Long ago in the village of Kessingland there stood a cinema that was quite unique. This is the intriguing story of the Kinnodrome and of Evered Wigg its proprietor, a man with a touch of genius whose life became an eccentric and colourful drama of invention and showmanship; but who was constantly dogged by bad luck. As well as building his own cinema and theatre, he was always creating his own inventions, which often found him 'back at the drawing board'.

Trained in electro–mechanics at a German university, he went into business in radio, meeting Marconi who gave him some of his patents to work on. It was at this time that Evered claimed to have had a breakthrough in his experimentation and could have invented television - but did he?

George Evered Wigg was born into the Wigg family of Barnby on Sept 6th 1878. His father William and his uncles ran the family firm, an agricultural machine suppliers and foundry works unsurprisingly named Wigg's of Barnby, which began trading in 1802 and, run by descendants, was still trading successfully until comparatively recently.

He was the result of William's second marriage, to one Amelia Beecroft, his first wife's best friend. It was his late wife's wish that he marry Amelia after her death. Between them they produced four more offspring, (William already being a father of six by his first marriage) George, Welbourne, Bertha and Edith, making William a father to ten children.

We will, from now on, refer to George as Evered, as he preferred to be

Beccles Free School in the late 19th Century

addressed by his middle name His little joke on the matter was: "Yes, I'd rather be called Evered, it's a bit different, you know. Every Tom, Dick and Harry is called George."

The absent-mindedness that followed Evered throughout life manifested itself at an early age. He used to relate a tale that in the good old days when everything was sold loose and all you needed was a container, his mother sent her 'Little Evvie' to the local grocery store for a jug of treacle. The shopkeeper having filled the jug, Evered was left searching high and low for the money with which to pay him. It was only later that he remembered that his mother, knowing full well what he was like, had put the money inside the jug for safe keeping.

Evered attended Beccles Free School, as it was then called, where in his own words, he was "far from being an exceptional pupil" but school reports show him at least to be a reasonable one. Frequent fights, and visits to the Headmaster's office for admonishment rather spoiled things. "I was seen to be a bit of a tearaway at times. Just a young fool, really – certainly no angel - better at fighting than writing" The school, situated in Ballygate, Beccles, is now the town's museum.

As a young schoolboy, Evered was fascinated by the boys' adventure comics available at the time, especially the artwork, which he avidly copied. He went on to create his own art and then cartoon strip stories. He was particularly interested in space themes, and travelling the deep ocean, and avidly consumed Jules Verne's *Twenty Thousand Leagues Under the Sea*, dreaming up his own themes whereby invention was given fertile ground within his prolific imaginings. He loved particularly the futuristic elements the stories contained and dreamed of being one day able to embark on such adventures himself – and added his own inventions to those within the publications he read. One of them was for a helmet which enabled a man to breathe underwater.. There were other inventions too, drawn in the form of diagrams in exercise books as a result of Evered's imaginings given stimulus by his readings. Did any of them work? No one will ever know.

He was always fascinated by geometric shapes. As he learned about them at school, he made his own, larger three – dimensional versions from cardboard and put them up in his bedroom, also making puzzles, (some of them very complex) out of odd pieces of wood which he found around his father's workshops. He also made his own puppets, along with a miniature stage, and would perform little playlets to any group of people who were interested in watching them.

When somewhat older, he developed an interest in the then new science of electronics, and read books written by physicists such as Sir William Crookes, who had recently developed the Crookes Tube – an early precursor of the television tube - and works by Sir Oliver Lodge, who was involved with the developing science of wireless telegraphy

He was also interested in Nikola Tesla, a physicist, inventor and acknowledged genius, who worked on the development of the light bulb and also, amongst other things is now accredited with inventing radio transmission and the universal installation of AC Current as a means of mains supply. By this his time, it was possible to see the sort of man that Evered might grow up to be. "The child", as some sage remarked, "is father to the man".

Evered's absent–mindedness was legendary. He travelled to school with his young brother Paul in a small pony trap, which, along with the pony, was kept near to the house for convenience to serve as a family runabout. On

Wiggs of Barnby

one particular day, Evered had all but arrived at school when he suddenly noticed that Paul wasn't there. Panicking, he went back and found his little brother crying but unhurt, having fallen off the cart! Evered scooped him back in, and they continued their journey to school.

Having duly left school, he decided to attend Leesburg University in Germany. "I told the family I thought it would be good for me," said Evered. "I would experience living in a different culture, and learn another language." He duly left school and on his family's agreement soon found himself studying electro–mechanical engineering at Leesburg University He had expressed to them the view that, having so far not travelled not much further than Barnby or Beccles he would like the opportunity to study abroad, feeling that it would be a very good way to increase his experience of life.

He did fairly well at his studies, made several friends, learned to speak the language passably well, and all in all the experience was a good one for him Returning to England, he continued his training in Birmingham for one year, sometimes feeling uncertain about his future in spite of the relative security which his background brought him.

Back at Barnby and still feeling restless he took a marathon cycle ride to Lincolnshire in an attempt to find work there. He felt himself to be the black (or at least the odd) sheep of the family – and knew in his bones that he would never really fit in to the way of life required to take over the family business which at some point he would be expected to do.

His father had high hopes that he could make a go of the new haulage section of the business recently developed by Wigg's. They had become suppliers of steam-powered traction engines made by Messrs. Elliot and Garroods of Leiston. Wigg's had taken out a contract to sell their steam engines, and they sold very well. They decided to purchase two of these machines for their own use, and to hire them out, complete with driver, for those who did not wish to incur the expense of purchasing one. As Evered was very interested in these engines and enjoyed working with them, the Wiggs furnished him with complete operating instructions, and sent him out on his first haulage assignment. After travelling a couple of hundred yards down the road to the sound of agonised grindings, the traction engine came to an abrupt halt. This seemed to be due to a total absence of water in the boiler, an oversight for which Evered was to blame. The traction engine - a very expensive item - was, of course, totally wrecked.

It seemed increasingly obvious to his family that he was patently unsuitable material to eventually run the family firm. In other words, they were coming to agree with his own feelings on the matter! After this episode, he was put in the charge of one John Bezant, the workshop foreman, a highly skilled man, who Evered's father thought would give him a thorough grounding in all aspects of workshop activity, and thus equip him with the knowledge to later take over the business He did lathe turning and casting in the foundry, where Wiggs, amongst other things made components for the railways, including several of the large round buffers which were placed between the carriages.

On Evered's father's insistence, Bezant set him a stringent standard of workmanship which at first Evered despaired of ever reaching. Later, he said: "He cast many of my castings back into the inferno, and whatever I did to improve matters, it still seemed to remain the same, but eventually, I seemed to reach the approved standard, as far more of them were kept and used." But for all that, Bezant was an amiable enough character and he and Evered got on well enough. Bezant invited him over to his cottage, where he spent his spare time making various model animals from leftovers of wood and metal. Evered loved the skill with which Bezant displayed in making these models, and referred to them as the 'silent menagerie.'

World War One: A Dark Cloud over the Nation

In 1909 Evered married his wife Gertrude (always known as Gertie) and for a while they settled in Barnby, with Evered still employed by his father. With his incredible energy, he built houses for key workers – the works manager and suchlike – and one for his brother Paul. One of the houses he worked on can still be seen as at least partly his handiwork owing to the unique windows it displays. This rather nice–looking house is situated across the road from the Wigg family home. He worked at this and other things for his father until suddenly there were rumblings of a possible impending war with Germany.

Within a short time this became a certainty, dark clouds of war loomed over the heads of the populace, and conscription was introduced. Evered at 36 would normally have been too old to consider joining up, but as the Government had recently raised the age to 42 he dutifully did so, joining the Naval Air Service, (a precursor of the RAF). After six weeks training, he was put in the carpentry shop, but as much as he had enjoyed carpentry in the past, he was, in his own words, finding this work of a "somewhat ignominious nature".

He applied for a transfer and found himself drafted to the dockyard at Felixtowe, where there was now a Seaplane Experimental Station. Evered found this far more to his liking. He helped finish a seaplane known as the Porte FB2, which was designed by one John Cyril Porte. It arrived in due course at Felixtowe to be finished and was given a trial run. It was, as it turned out, a total failure. Nicknamed 'The Baby', it seemed to have very little power, and could only take off in a strong wind. It spent most of its time sitting in its launching cradle in a hanger.

"Porte Baby" F2A flying boat

Porte then came up with another version with some modification, which became known as the Porte Super Baby. This model, equipped with a more powerful engine, (and some modifications suggested by Evered) actually flew! Evered assisted with these for about ten months, until they had built a small fleet of them. Cumbersome by today's, standards, they looked more like flying boats than seaplanes, and seemed to have had all the aerodynamics of a bumblebee! They were mainly used for reconnaissance purposes.

Gertie, of course, had moved with him, and whilst at at Felixtowe their cottage caught the full impact of German bombs, and Gertie saved their little daughter Greta by rushing into the blazing building and dragging her out. They were both unhurt. Afterwards they lived for a while in emergency accommodation, namely an army hut near to the docks, as did a number of other families whose houses had been rendered unfit to live in after the air–raid.

Soon after, Evered had his first chance to work on something more in line with his greatest interest and training – that of electro mechanical engineering. A communications device arrived at the base, and out of the large number of men asked if they knew anything about devices of this nature only Evered raised his hand. Valve – powered equipment at this time was quite a new thing, It was a huge box – basically an early valve radio with correspondingly huge valves, condensers etc. Smallness and compactness related to any invention always seem to develop later. He worked on it all one day, and managed to get it to operate well enough. However, apart from running it through tests, he never saw it in action, for the day after, he was transferred to Kent where he worked at Manston and various other naval stations, It is not really known how he spent the rest of the war, but it is believed that he flew as a tail–gunner, and flying over Germany, was thought to have dropped several bombs on the towns and cities of the enemy.

Evered hated this war, and was inherently pacifistic, feeling that he should really have been a Conscientious Objector. The problem for him was that for his time at Leesburg, he had lived and studied with the German people, had developed great friendships with some of his fellow students and considered them to be his kinsmen. Now overnight, due to this war these erstwhile friends had overnight become enemies, and when dropping bombs from planes over Germany, on buildings and over German trenches, Evered sometimes wondered how many of his former colleagues he had inadvertently killed. – a sad, paradoxical situation.

Victory for Britain: the End of the War

Evered was demobbed in 1919, and arrived back in Barnby with his wife and child, glad to be no longer involved, as he saw it, in this "seemingly endless stupidity of war". He took up residence in one of the firm's cottages but Evered was feeling even less keen to resume work at his father's firm, and even more of an outsider after fighting in the war. For a while he resumed his duties, but working in the foundry reminded him of the horrific images that he had seen in wartime. It made him feel nauseous, and he found he could no longer do it. His family had by this time came to understand that the war had left Evered quite badly traumatised and he was put on light duties, did odd jobs around the premises, and also helped care for his mother, who had been disabled in a motoring accident in 1902. He was given plenty of time to rest and pursue his own activities which, of course, was the objective.

Before long, with the aid of two thousand pound legacy left him by his father, who died in 1915, he decided to move and pursue a dream of his own, and after a fair amount of searching, the place he chose to move to was Kessingland. The Kessingland which Evered choose to move to was a very different place from what one sees today. The centre of Kessingland consisted of a large farm which now is a sprawl of houses, there are also houses on many miscellaneous pieces of land which used to be fields and meadows; indeed it seems that every available scrap of land has been colonised by property developers.

Back then, longshore boats proliferated on the beach, and Kessingland had been renowned as a rich fishing village since the Middle Ages. Many earned

Fisherman's Gap, Kessingland, in the early 20th century

a living from fishing or related industries. Or, if not, they usually worked on a farm. There are now no boats on the beach. In those days , the sea was but a short walk from the sea wall, now if you set out to walk to the sea, due to some strange shift in land-mass, you will need to walk some quarter of a mile to reach your destination. Most of the farm land is now covered by houses, and a population of approximately 400 prior to the mid 1960s have now grown to over 4,000. Needless to say, the farming community has gone and the milking byre near to the church, which once served a thriving dairy herd, is now derelict and overgrown with weeds.

Sir Henry Rider–Haggard, the prolific novelist and traveller, author of amongst several other works, *King Solomon's Mines* and *She*, bought a property on Kessingland cliffs in 1900 called Cliff Grange and renamed it Kessingland Grange. Kessingland and neighbouring villages such as Pakefield on the East Coast had experienced horrific amounts of coastal erosion and many properties had slid over the edge of the cliffs after a series of terrific storms, and were lost. Sir Henry decided to take action in an attempt to ameliorate this. Using the prodigious knowledge of horticulture he had gained whilst out in Africa, he planted at his own expense a large quantity of marram grass all along the beach.

The great thing about marram grass is that its roots are very successful in binding sand together, and after the marram became established and was growing healthily, the devastation caused by coastal erosion was much

Kessingland Grange, Home of Sir Henry Rider-Haggard

reduced. To take such an action was partly in Sir Henry's interest as his own property was at risk.

Following his death in 1925, the Grange was sold and in 1928 it became the property of a Mr Catchpole, who turned the grounds into an early holiday camp for those who wished to have a break from the hurly-burly of city life. The house was subsequently demolished in order to extend the park. The path which leading up to the clifftops where the Grange once stood in all its finery is to this day known as Rider Haggard Lane. Incidentally he was visited on odd occasions by Rudyard Kipling, whom the locals regarded with great suspicion. They most probably did not know who he was, but considered that anyone with a Rolls–Royce and such a huge moustache must be up to no good - but that's the locals for you!

Evered purchased a property, a big, rambling old house located just off the A12 at Kessingland, which he christened Glen Cairn, apparently after being captivated by a place of the same name whilst honeymooning in the Scottish highlands. It was here in the grounds of this house that he began to build the Kinnodrome. People must have wondered at the strange building taking shape along the main London road as you entered Kessingland and when Evered told some people that he was building a cinema there, some did not believe him Built over a fairly long period, the Kinnodrome was constructed mainly from parts salvaged from old wooden buildings, supplemented by the occasional visit to builders` merchants.

Evered endeavoured to work on the most economical budget he knew how,

The Coxswain and his boat, 1908

therefore it also utilised such materials as old brass bedsteads and strange and lovely old pieces of wrought ironwork which he probably salvaged from local scrapyards. The box–office he bought complete from an old theatre which was being demolished – giving it, as he put it an "afterlife". The sum total of all this was that partly the materials used, and partly Evered being in charge of its design lead to this little theatre having a quirky, somewhat bizarre look.

In the midst of all this, Evered took steps to pursue another long-nurtured dream, which was to own and operate a mobile film show and theatre, partly to take these things to people who lived deep in the countryside and had few facilities, and with a view to visiting schools and performing shows which the children could participate in – in fact, a part of his Happy Neighbours Theatre theme. In order to achieve this, he took the train to London, and purchased a lorry. This antediluvian conveyance sported solid tyres and oil lamps, and decided to take him about half the way home, after which distance it produced a series of grinding noises, and thereafter refused to budge. Evered eventually got this contraption home and had it repaired, only to find that a short while later, the Government announced that all vehicles with solid tyres were now illegal on Britain's roads. Costing a thousand pounds – a huge sum of money in those days – this left a sizeable hole in Evered's budget. He later described it as 'the most expensive garden ornament he had ever purchased '- it stood at the side of one of the sheds at the Kinnodrome, and generations of small boys had great fun playing 'drivers 'on it. Evered never drove a vehicle again, instead sticking to his trusty bicycle.

A Bizarre Cinema

The Kinnodrome is Completed

The First Film Show

As the Kinnodrome slowly grew, it began more and more to reflect the eccentric nature of its owner, as he painted it every colour under the sun and festooned the frontage overlooking the main road with lettering and carvings, many of a strange and highly symbolic nature. It was eventually finished and on a fine Saturday morning in May, Evered held a well–publicized Grand Opening Day with Wrentham Town Band, who were hired to play the occasion in. At exactly twelve noon, the band struck up, and as they did so, a drawbridge–like contraption, a sort of gantry, dropped down from high up in the front gable–end of the building, and onto this Evered walked, complete with megaphone, and proceeded to address the assembled masses. A long, droning speech followed, after which after which tea, lemonade and buns were served inside the newly-completed building. The assembled crowd filed in, carrying their expectations with them – and looking forward to the evening and the first film showing at the Kinnodrome.

Thus the first film showing in the Kinnodrome that evening took place – and what a show! Evered had spent a considerable sum of money on projectors and other equipment and had, as explained previously, wasted a large sum of money on a lorry which was no earthly good, and stood no chance of bringing him any sort of income. The outcome of all this was that Evered had been unable to complete the Kinnodrome by installing a wooden floor and fitted seats with an aisle, and instead the audience, much their amusement, found themselves to be sitting on deckchairs and

The Kinnodrome in later years

benches on the grass inside the Kinnodrome! Eventually, when the Kingdome's budget allowed, Evered installed a proper floor, fitted seats and an aisle. Amongst all this excitement, Greta gave birth to Tony, and then Peter. Evered and Gertie were now the proud parents of three children; and Greta had two brothers.

For a while, Evered's most successful venture was in the cinema business. Greats such as Buster Keaton, Chaplin, Laurel and Hardy and many others adorned the cinema screens. There was also a character little heard of these days who might be said to be a cinematic forerunner of Tarzan, who had yet to grace the silver screen. He was known as Elmo the Mighty and each Saturday morning crowds of excited children arrived at the Kinnodrome to see his next jungle adventure, literally a cliffhanger! In the following episode he was miraculously rescued by an elephant whilst Gertie pounded out melodramatic accompaniment on the piano.

She was an infinite source of support in most of his projects, and as well asproviding the music she worked in the ticket office, and even made the ice-cream to sell to cinema-goers during the interval! However, love and appreciate her as he obviously did, there were times when Evered needed to get away – there were times, he claimed, when she nagged him quite a lot - and for times like this he had a bolt –hole. Somewhere in the middle of the Kinnodrome a trap-door hung suspended by a series of ropes and pulleys. He would sit on this trap – door and pull himself up into the false ceiling, thus effecting his escape. As far as anyone knows she never discovered his hiding place........

Even during those days of silent film shows , there was some form of Health and Safety inspection and one day, soon after it was built, two of their officers called to examine the Kinnodrome. "This building is made of wood", one of them exclaimed. "You entertain several members of the public here, and as far as I can see, there is no kind of emergency exit. What if there was a fire on the premises? What would you do?"

"Come with me" said Evered, and walking to the far wall, pulled a lever. With that, the whole side of the Kinnodrome lifted up.! As for the safety inspectors – what could they say? Wartime images of people burning to death had left Evered worried about fire, and he was the first to make sure that adequate precautions against it were taken.

The main thing which facilitated early cinemas was the invention by the Lumiere brothers of the Cinematographe. Brothers from France, they took a great interest in their father's work. An award winning photographer, in 1870 he moved his family from the hazardous Eastern border to the city of Lynn. Also a portrait painter, he opened a small business in photographic plates in his new home. Two of his sons, Augustine and Louis grew up fascinated by his work. Later, they worked on an invention, One year later, the brothers had succeeded and the Luminaire Chronograph had been patented. This remarkable invention could record, develop and project film.

Remarkably, although the brothers were clever and insightful in their inventing they could see no future for it. – Louis, shortly after their first public showing of moving film was said to have remarked, "le cinema est. invention sans avenir" ("Cinema is an invention without a future"). How wrong could he been! It revolutionised entertainment – making cinemas such as Evered's a possibility.

The Gaumont Chronograph was probably a somewhat simplified {and therefore cheaper} version of the Luminaire Brothers' invention. It was a projector only, having no other facility but to project moving pictures. To have such a place as the Kinnodrome in a small village like Kessingland must certainly have been a novelty, especially in the days when there was little else in the way of entertainment and a new film or show advertised on the hoardings was usually greeted with much interest by the locals. Antiquated by modern standards, the projection system at the Kinnodrome used the technology of the day. Acetylene was manufactured in a large drum at the back of the Kinnodrome, which before the widespread use of electricity provided the lighting for the interior of the building as well as for the projector.

As with any projector, light was shone from the back through a series of lenses, which then picked up the moving frames, casting them onto the screen, creating an animated effect. The main difference was that in those days the film was cranked through by hand-quite laborious processes by all accounts! This equipment would break down at frequent intervals and when it did, Evered in his eccentric way, would take off his jacket and perform somersaults down the aisle. He also had a set of juggling balls which he could use with some skill. There was, however, some method in his madness. The main objective being to keep audiences (particularly children) from becoming bored and walking out which, Evered felt would do little to enhance the reputation of the Kinnodrome.

This projection system was known as the Cinematograph, which, incidentally, is the origin of the word cinema. Occasionally a boy was employed to turn the handle in return for a free ticket. Due to lack of experience (or perhaps mischief), the film would sometimes be wound through at hilariously exaggerated speeds, for example an approaching motor cycle might be whisked through with breakneck speed, for example in a scenario where cowboys were staging a duel the film might be wound through with agonising slowness, giving rise to considerable mirth amongst the audience. Due to rust spots in a corrugated iron roof people found they could be dripped on when it was raining outside, so some would take umbrellas or sou'westers to a film show just in case. When it rained it must have hit the tin roof with a deafening noise!

The Kinnodrome also catered for travelling repertory companies and quite a number of these performed plays there. There were also assorted acts such as singers, comedians and jugglers whose names have not survived as most of them were lesser known and never made it to the halls of fame. However, one of the more memorable is the Lady in Red. Dressed in red from head to foot she sang, danced, played the piano and performed monologues. Off stage she still wore her red outfits and as she lodged in the village whilst performing at the Kinnodrome she could be seen on occasions riding about on a bicycle-which was also red. In fact, the only thing about her that wasn't red was her monologues!

Shows Inside and Out

During the summer the grounds of the Kinnodrome were turned over to the travelling fairs. There were several of them and they flourished, as forms of entertainment though were far more limited than they are today. All the old fairground effects were here, freak shows, fire-eaters, strong man acts and of course, the inevitable rides such as steam-powered roundabouts, swing boats and carousels. Amongst the more eccentric of these sideshows was "Lift the Fat Lady" who must have weighed over twenty stones. If you succeeded in lifting her you won a prize, you could then go on to guess the weight you had lifted, with the chance of winning yet another prize (to go with your hernia?).

In the meantime Evered 'passion for inventing continued. He drew up plans for a bending caravan, which duly materialised in his workshop. The device pre-dated the Bendibus, which came on the scene much later, but was similar as it sported a swivelling chassis. Perhaps Evered should have invented a bus! Although he patented this device and forwarded it to several firms, strangely enough none of them wanted to go into production with it. It had a wooden cabin and was enormous, apparently aimed at the person who went camping in a big way! Eventually Evered abandoned any ambitions he might have had for this invention and went on to other things, and it stood at the side of the Kinnodrome, filled with junk, and forgotten. He also invented a shoe shining machine - a contraption contrived from cycle parts - but he claimed that Cherry Blossom shoe polish, then a recent invention, offered too much competition, and therefore this invention was also abandoned.

A considerable time before the ballpoint pen had been invented he had another great idea. He distributed a pen he had invented amongst friends and neighbours. With the outer casing made from bamboo it was about three inches in length and sealed with an oversized wooden ball on top on which were inscribed the immortal words *Scripto Ad Infinitum* Had anyone taken him seriously, Evered might indeed have made his fortune with this invention. As a youngster I was a recipient of one of these pens, and over the years it has had constant use, I even used it through college and when starting to write this book I took it out and tried it and yes, it still writes! As with the pen, Evered never pursued any idea long enough to ensure its success, and was instead constantly flitting from one madcap invention to another.

Bad fortune overtook the Kinnodrome in the shape of the silent films being rapidly replaced by those with sound tracks. Cinemas were springing up in nearby Lowestoft and offered films with the newly – contrived sound track, plus the relative luxury of not having to bring an umbrella in case ir rained! This (former) dismayed Evered, as he disliked these new "talkies," claiming that they marred the intrinsic spirit of film, which in his view was about body language and mime. On a more practical level, he found that he could not afford the relatively expensive equipment needed to screen these modern films. Without an income from his film shows he was finding it increasingly difficult to afford to pay his performing artistes, so before long the inevitable happened and the Kinnodrome ceased, at least for the time being, to be a centre for the performing arts.

The Radio Years: Meeting with Marconi

After this, the ever-enterprising Evered picked up an earlier interest and again put the Kinnodrome to good use by forming a partnership with his brother Paul and beginning again to build radios. Now, radios were mainly valve sets and on the general market were very expensive, but Evered and Paul could make them at a much cheaper price than this- even making the cabinets in which they were housed! They also repaired radios, made their own two-way radios for customers on request, and repaired telephones and anything of this nature that might come their way. The brothers built up a good business – in fact the most successful enterprise the Kinnodrome had ever seen!

At this time Evered visited London during one of the exhibitions held at Crystal Palace These mainly featured technological advances, and it was here that he met Marconi, The two men discussed extensively the uses of radio, and also experimentation concerned with extending its uses. To all intents and purposes they got along well, as Marconi offered some of his patents to work on, to Evered's great delight! Returning home, he took Marconi's patents with him, and diligently set to work.

Evered went on to spend the next few years pottering about the Kinnodrome, making this or that on the lathes and other machinery which he had in his workshop. There was no electricity in the Kinnodrome, and all the equipment was made by Evered and mostly powered by bicycle peddles and belts and flywheels, and of course by Evered himself. Amongst other things, each time he heard of a newly married couple in the village he would make the bride a rolling - pin as a wedding present. Oh how times have changed! But he did not stop there. He could make just about anything he thought someone might buy. Wooden bowls, toys shelves, and bookcases were all made. He cast concrete blocks, and made some money by selling these. Interestingly, he sometimes cast concrete so that it had the appearance of glass. No-one ever learned how he did this, but here, I suspect, is something that had it been put forward in the form of a patent, might have attracted the attention of manufactures, and was, for Evered, perhaps yet another potential opportunity which came to nothing, and was sold only for modest amounts of money.

It was while doing this he constantly visited a local builder to obtain sand, cement and shingle in order to cast his concrete blocks. Evered and his squeaky old wheelbarrow became a familiar sight to the builder. He used to craze the man by droning on and on about this or that, and on this occasion he was in the builder's office, putting forward an idea to cure the leaks in the Kingdome's roof. This he proposed to do by clambering up on the roof, and, armed with a collection of lead rivets, hold these down with a heavy hammer, while the builder climbed a ladder, and riveted them in place, thus curing the leaks. The builder refused. He thought the idea ill – advised and rather dangerous. But while he went on and on, the builder noticed that\Evered kept shrugging his shoulders, and lifting the collar of his jacket. Suddenly, a privet hawk moth emerged from the collar of his jacket, and flew to the window, Privet hawk moths are huge – the largest moth in the British Isles! To this day, no – one knows whether this was some sort of unique conjuring trick or simply that Evered had left his jacket in the Kinnodrome for a while, and a caterpillar had decided to crawl inside and pupate. It became an anecdote told endlessly in the local pub by the builder.

Over the years, Evered continued adding to the lettering and general décor that helped make the Kinnodrome the striking sight it was. There were all kinds of geometric shapes, some being frames which contained mirrors and large turned wooden balls which stood on posts. On the wrought-iron perimeter railings were more strange shapes, including the carvings of animals executed in bass relief by his father's old foreman John Bezant. Everything was painted in the vivid colours of a fairground. He took possession of some of the model animals after Bezant's death, and used them at a later date for his own décor at the Kinnodrome, where they could be seen for long years after, adorning the front fence. At the end of the building was the Olaf Gate, apparently named after King Olaf of Norway. This royal personage, Evered claimed, had once walked through here whilst on a visit to the area. Nobody in the village can ever remember this visit taking place; if King Olaf visited the Kinnodrome, he practiced an incredible degree of modesty for a king!

The Carrebar denoted a piece of equipment invented by Evered's grandfather for pouring molten iron from the smelting works of a foundry during the casting process. The Carrebar was Shown at the Great Exhibition of 1865, Evered was very proud of his grandfather's invention and it seemed that he was a major source of inspiration to Evered, and certainly seemed to be a major influence in the desire to invent that he retained throughout his life. Evered displayed its name on the Kinnodrome in large letters naming his business the Carrebar Company.

Actually, the Carrebar is worthy of a bit more attention – not so much as a great invention, but it serves to illustrate very well the total lack of safety and disregard for human life that Victorian industrialists had for their employees. If it was ever in use, the Carrebar was a yoked device which enabled one man to carry on his shoulders two pots of molten metal, front and rear, and what was likely to happen if a man, probably wearing little in the way of protective clothing ever slipped on a floor likely to be oily, whilst carrying two pots of molten metal – I shudder to think!

The Four H's was a beautifully intertwined carving symbolising Happiness, Health, Honesty and Humanity — these to Evered were the four cardinal virtues and according to him any task if it was to be done well was best undertaken by four people. In Evered's perception, it would then be "a balanced task" A sign in brightly painted wooden lettering along the top of the Kinnodrome read *Foursome*, and endorsed this idea.

At the time Evered was running a printing press in the Kinnodrome from which he earned a small income by producing business and other cards to order. His own business card was interesting. Printed on his press, it read, left to right Cake of Cruz, Bond of Bruz, Arc of Amaz, and Erie of Amaz This I think most people would agree this must be one of the most extraordinary business cards ever. Where he came across such terms and what they actually mean is anybody's guess. Perhaps King Olaf schooled him in Nordic legend! The outside of the Kinnodrome was festooned with such unique words.

Another of his fascinations was radio. Starting with the crystal set which first came on the scene in the early twentieth century, he graduated to valve radio when that became available, buying the components and building them from scratch. It was on one of the radio sets in his workshop that he had built in a previous time he first heard Chamberlain declare that Britain was in a state of war with Germany. Being the sort of man he was he took it upon himself to inform the good people of Kessingland, some no doubt without radios, of this all-important announcement. This he did with the aid of his trusty old bicycle and a megaphone. He then went home, boarded up the Kinnodrome and raised the Union Jack on a flagpole situated in the grounds, whilst playing the National Anthem on an old wind-up gramophone with a large brass horn.

Having done his considered duty he left the building, daubing hastily on it the words in whitewash: WORLD WAR HAS CAUSED INEVITABLE CLOSURE OF THESE PREMISES. HOPE TO RE-OPEN AFTER. IF BUILDING STILL STANDING! Poor old Evered - In the excitement he had forgotten that the Kinnodrome had already been closed! Soon after this, Evered joined the war effort as a pattern maker in a local shipyard as war took hold on the country and the Kinnodrome fell into disrepair. The painted notice remained long after the war ended, indeed. it remained, pale and faded but still legible, right up until the building was demolished!

One summer in the mid-1950s after years of standing neglected, the Kinnodrome was suddenly galvanised into activity by Evered's announcement that the Grand Solotogo Event was to be held in the Kinnodrome on one Saturday morning, and several people arrived out of curiosity, Evered mounted the stage and proceeded to deliver a speech to the effect that Solotogo was a board game which he and a Colonel Anderson of the U.S. Army, whom he had met during the war years, had devised together. It was a community game, said Evered, which he hoped would rival bingo in popularity and eventually as it spread, would help prevent further wars as international games would encourage unity between nations.

The speech droned on, ending eventually in an announcement that the first

Solotogo "drive" would be taking place at 7.30 that evening. The first Solotogo drive took place as promised at 7.30 pm. Before it began the assembled masses were required to stand and sing "Oh Solo, Solotogo" to the tune of "The Hokey Cokey" before they took delivery of their Solotogo boards and started to play. Thus Solotogo was born. Unfortunately for Evered the main drawback with Solotogo was simply that nobody really understood it! For a few months people turned up for games but more for the fun of being there and singing the Solotogo song and the tea and buns at the interval than anything else. Far more complex than bingo, it was incomprehensible to the average person while some said they thought it to be a mixture of chess and draughts As with many things to do with Evered - nobody really knew!

Before long the populace tired of it and stopped coming to the games and sadly, Solotogo died a death. After it failed as a community game, he simplified it and adapted it as a road safety game for families He wrote to the then Minister of Transport, Ernest Marples, outlining his ideas but obtained little support from him, and sadly, like the rest of his inventions Solotogo soon became cast to one side, forgotten and gon.

Over the years Evered continued adding to the lettering and general décor that helped make the Kinnodrome what it was. There were all kinds of geometric shapes, some being frames which contained mirrors and large turned wooden balls which stood on posts. The wooden balls were characteristic of Evered's handiwork On the wrought-iron perimeter railings lurked yet more mysterious shapes. The section of theatre in which Evered invited people in general to participate was called "Happy Neighbours" and hosted amateur theatre nights in which all could be involved. Needless to say, great fun was had by all! The main objective of the Happy Neighbours Theatre was, according to Evered, 'to bring happiness to the lives of children', and I am sure that this was something which at least to a certain degree, it succeeded in doing.

Evered, never lost his optimism, despite his many setbacks and was ever looking forward, and for that amongst other things, I admire him.

Did Evered Wigg Invent Television?

This is more debatable than most people may think. He used to claim that he had, amidst a general attitude of ridicule. But, bear in mind that most people probably did not have a full knowledge of his background. However, those with a better knowledge of his activities know that Evered was experimenting with radio when he met Marconi, and he let him have some of his patents, and invited them to expand them, which he did with experimental work, and his customary enthusiasm. One day, in 1925 he made his breakthrough. He excitedly contacted Marconi and told him the good news, saying "My lifelong dream is on the way to coming true – electric pictures!" Evered had offered to go into partnership with Marconi – and he provisionally agreed on the strength of them coming up with something substantial on which they could all work, and waned to discuss this in some detail. Evered proposed they call this wonderful new device the Carrebar Telivisor.

Then, Paul was suddenly taken ill, and in 1928 to Evered's great sorrow after a short period of illness, he died. Evered felt no incentive to carry on alone – he was devastated by his younger brother's death and for a considerable time did little. Developments on the television breakthrough were of course not followed up, and sadly there it was – yet another abandoned project. Marconi could not have been pleased. While the waited, the television was invented and patented by an independent party.

Later Years

Probably the last thing that Evered spent his time creating was The Delf — a grotto behind the Kinnodrome. Cut partly into the bank, the whole area was floored with mosaic tiling depicting designs and wording. A chess set with pieces about three feet in height was let into the general mosaic in black and white tiling. In order to play with this massive set it was necessary to tilt the pieces and roll them about the board. At the sides of the Delf there were curved and beautifully carved seats to sit on. But now, few people came to the Kinnodrome.but life had never stood still for long for Evered.

Groups of hippies, no doubt attracted by the strange quality of the place, began to visit. On summer evenings, groups of them hearing tales of old film and invention would arrive in old trucks, longhaired and exotically garbed, to gather together and "share the experience." Evered enjoyed their company, becoming quite a local guru. And for a short time, the Kinnodrome enjoyed a minor revival, as the hippies tried to learn and play Solotogo, sat in the Delf and smoked their weird cigarettes He inspired their art – and they probably his. "Interesting, I think they understand my work" said he.

One of Evered's sayings was "A man learns something each day" and on this particular day, he was introduced quite belatedly to motor-cycles. He had reached the bus-stop a little late, and had missed the bus, when the local Rockers, who knew Evered, decided to give him a lift. He climbed on the back; the rider wound back the throttle, and the motor-bike sailed along at 90 mph. As they reached their destination, the boy was wondering whether he should have gone quite so fast with his elderly passenger but, when they came to a stop, Evered jumped from the back, looking rather flushed, but unfazed. "That was wonderful" he said, adding that the best part was missing the bus, and then passing it again along the way!

Evered pottered around for another few years enjoying life, always optimistic, always seeking that ultimate invention until he passed away quite suddenly at the age of ninety one, bringing an abrupt end to any activity at the Kinnodrome. For a few more years it stood, paint peeling, an abandoned and ghostly hulk, like some faithful old dog that had lost its master. It really did seem that, on Evered's passing it had lost something. Then Gertie also died and the premises were eventually sold. The Kinnodrome was demolished to make way for a factious little housing estate serving to line the pockets of property developers. There is now no trace of the Kinnodrome or any of the things that went along with it - The Lady in Red, the Fat Lady, the Strong Man, the steam roundabout, the swing boats the queues for the cinema to see Elmo the Mighty, and a whole host of other things and characters. They are now ghosts living only in the memory, and Evered was again there with them.

Evered Wigg was a unique character; I grew up in Kessingland and have personal memories of him as do several others, and would like to share the experience of Evered Wigg and the Kinnodrome with others, which is the reason that I wrote this book.

Postscript: Cyril Porte

After WW1 had ended, all that Porte, Evered and the rest of the team had done to develop the new concept of flying boats had come to an end, and indeed had by 1920 reached a state of total obscurity with the demolition of the sheds in which they had carried out their research. The specially-adapted quay on which they had put their discoveries to the test was converted back to a conventional quay, and so reverted back to being a mooring-place for freight vessels. It is surprising that the flying boats and all surrounding them were not valued more, as they made a large contribution to the war effort, and continued research and development could have lead to major discoveries being made.

Years passed, and it was not until 1978 that two of the seaplane's components were actually recognised for what they were - namely the large nose cones that they sported were discovered and brought to the museum,. One had been in a private garden where it had for years been used as a potting shed. The other stood in the field at a local football club, where it had been used as a changing for footballers! At almost the same time, by strange coincidence, John Cyril Porte's grave, neglected and overgrown, was discovered in London, where he had spent the rest of his life. On the headstone, after cleaning, it could be seen that Porte was once hailed as the inventor of flying boats.

Although he was invalided out of the Naval Service due to having pulmonary thrombosis in 1913, his active life was far from over. He came into contact with Glen Curtiss, an ambitious aircraft pioneer from America, and he travelled there to assist him on a number of projects, chiefly the

A Bristol Scout mounted on a Porte FB 2

design of a seaplane that could cross the Atlantic. As part of the agreement, Porte would receive a 20-25% commission on sales of the seaplanes he designed. Returning from the US on the outbreak of the War, Porte's agreement remained in place and it was arranged that these payments would be handled by a former barrister named William Casson for a commission.

In his role at Felixstowe, Porte was responsible for the purchase of seaplanes and ordered many from the Curtiss Company, duly receiving his commission from Casson, allegedly receiving £48,000 in this manner before this blatant conflict of interest was discovered. A trial took place at Bow Street Magistrates Court. On 19 November 1917 Casson admitted guilt but as he had returned the money, bar £10,000 which had already been spent and in light of his failing health and important war service, the Attorney General entered a *nolle prosequi* and the case did not proceed although Casson was fined for his part.

In 1922 Porte was recognised with an award from the Royal Commission on Awards to Inventors in relation to flying boats and later his widow received an award of £1500.00 from the Commission in respect of information passed to the US Government concerning inventions, designs, etc. in relation to aircraft and aircraft accessories, specifically flying Tragically, John Cyril Porte had died in 1919 at the age of only thirty five, due mainly to hard work in spite of his illness, but he was remembered as a hero.

Cyril Porte with a Curtiss Model H

Printed in Great Britain
by Amazon